LATER DATE
BY
TOMMY WILSON JR.

Later Date
by Tommy Wilson Jr. © 2023

ISBN-13: 978-1-947288-74-4

All rights reserved solely by the author. Unless otherwise indicated, the author certifies all contents are original and do not infringe upon the legal rights of any other person or work. No part of this book may be reproduced in any form without the written permission of the publisher. The views expressed in this book are not necessarily those of the publisher. Scripture quotations marked KJV are taken from the King James Version of the Bible. Scripture quotations marked NASB are taken from the New American Standard Bible®, Copyright © 1960, 1962, 1963, 1968, 1971, 1972, 1973, 1975, 1977, 1995 by The Lockman Foundation Used by permission." (www.Lockman.org). Scripture quotations marked NIV are taken from the NIV2011, New International Version®, **NIV**®. Copyright © 1973, 1978, 1984, 2011 by Biblica, Inc.™ Used by permission of Zondervan. All rights reserved worldwide. www.zondervan.com. Scripture quotations marked **NKJV**™ are taken from the New King James Version®. Copyright © 1982 by Thomas Nelson, Inc. Used by permission.

Printed in the United States
10 9 8 7 6 5 4 3 2 1

Cover design by: Octavius Holmes
www.ohstudiozcom
oyholmes80@gmail.com

Published by
Life To Legacy, LLC
P.O. Box 1239
Matteson, IL 60443
www.Life2Legacy.com
Life2legacybooks@att.net

Contents

Dedication	5
Introduction	7
Day 1	11
Day 2	14
Day 3	20
Day 4	24
Day 5	29
Day 6	33
Day 7	37
Day 8	40
Day 9	42
Day 10	45

Contents

Day 11 — 48

Day 12 — 51

Day 13 — 55

Day 14 — 59

Day 15 — 65

Day 16 — 68

Day 17 — 71

Day 18 — 75

Day 19 — 79

Day 20 — 90

Day 21 — 95

About the Author — 101

Dedication

This book is dedicated to many special people in my life who have all been a great source of support and encouragement to me concerning this book project, in ministry, and throughout my life. I could not be the man I am today without your prayers, love, and support and sincerely thank God for all of you.

To Cici, Jawan and Bralon, thank you for believing in me during the difficult times and encouraging me along the way.

To my mom Queen for accepting me back home when life turned upside down. She always said it's going to get better, and just as you said, it did.

To my siblings Henry, Eric, Katrina, Ava, and Al you all have a special place in my heart as you supported me all the way on my road to recovery. I give God thanks for your prayers, support and love that helped get me through.

To my best friend Donald, since sixth grade you were there for me during all of this turmoil. You always told me the truth and loved me like a brother. I thank you your wife Lisa for everything you did to guide me back to my rightful place in life.

To Walter and William, you are some good brothers who played key roles in my life. Walter was a catalyst to bridge certain gaps in my life that I needed badly at times. William helped me out in so many ways as well that only friends can do.

To my Apostle E. L. Usher, thank you for the wisdom and counsel you gave me in life, and for my book. Thank you so much for your love and support.

To First Lady Usher for the divine connection to the three-way call that started the talking between Sophia and me. Thank you for everything that you have done.

To Gerald Benton, thank you for your words of wisdom during this time. I appreciate your prayers and friendship.

To Prophet Marqus Beaver, you played a significant role in my life and truly you have been a huge inspiration to me.

To Apostle John Eckhardt thank you for your blessing on our union. Your wisdom and love will take us far.

I dedicate this book to all that have been knocked down but decided that wasn't your final destination. The champion in you had to come forth. I want to give a special dedication to my wife for believing in somebody like me who was down in life but chose to love in a way that only I needed.

And last but not least, to Sophia, I appreciate you so much and thanks for being my love.

Introduction

Many are probably wondering how I ended up writing a book. I never thought of myself as a writer, because I did not understand that one day, I would have something to share with others. Unwittingly, yet by divine appointment here I am, an author who was called to share my story to be a blessing to others. Now I understand that releasing a book is a two-way street. For the author writing it is cathartic and a pathway for healing. For the reader it is enlightenment and understanding through the impartation of experience and wisdom. Therefore, have written *Later Date* to tell my story about where I have been and all that I have been through. As you engage in my story, you will see there were many psychological and emotional struggles that I came through. Indeed, there were some deep pits in dark places. But thanks be to God, though it is darkest before the dawn, joy comes in the morning.

There are countless testimonial books on the market concerning relationships that have failed. Most of them have been written from the woman's perspective. However, this book is different, because it is my story written from a man's perspective. Hopefully this doesn't come as a surprise, but men have feelings too. We hurt, we cry, we get depressed, and we ask God, why. What do you do when you've done all you can, and your marriage still fails? You feel that devastating blow, like a TKO that sends your marriage down for the count. Before you know it, you're on a road that ends in divorce.

No couple gets married to end up in divorce court. We all have high hopes to live "happily ever after." Needless to say, when things go south and "for better or for worse" is not keeping you together, the tension gets unbearable, and the acrimony is worse. But I am a witness, the end is not yet. No matter how bad it gets, "trouble won't last always." This to, shall come to past. Therefore, I have come to encourage someone that even through all of the hurt and pain that a divorce will bring, with God's help you can learn to trust, love and live again. You'll get through it, by living through it.

Divorce is a hard pill to swallow. There is a lot of change that comes along with it. You have many mixed emotions. You grieve over what it lost, all the norms and routines that have been established, and known during that union change. In the aftermath of separation you must recalibrate everything. You have to get reacquainted with it just being you. You must learn to balance relief with loneliness. As I was going through my divorce, I couldn't see myself ever moving forward. Let alone ever getting married again. However, God knew, and He guided me through. I had to lean on Him and follow His direction.

It was necessary to write this book because it's important for me to help others understand that God can get you through every season of your life. If you trust Him, God will lead you step-by-step. While going through this process I learned some practical strategies that I believe will help someone. First of all, do not go into it alone. Talk to someone to whom you are safe sharing your feelings and experiences. Secondly, understand that you should not go through divorce trauma alone. You need to seek professional help by speaking to a therapist or seeking Godly counsel. This type of support really helped me. When you are going through separation is not a time to be macho. As men we often fall into the trap of suppressing our feelings and hide our vulnerabilities. But that's dangerous because whenever you're in a dark spot, you need some guiding light. Failure to seek counsel can result in bad things. Negative thoughts can take over that can lead to some ugly circumstances.

When you are hurting and angry, you are more vulnerable to giving in to ungodly thoughts that cross your mind. If you are not careful you will find yourself sinking deeper and deeper into a dark pit of despair. That's when you find yourself feeling hopeless. You have to speak to someone, and you have to get it out. It's good for the soul. It's good for your heart. It's good for everyone around you, especially your immediate circle, your family, and your kids.

Even though divorce is between a husband and wife, but it impacts everyone around them. The Children are watching. They see everything and they are usually terrified. My children needed a lot of reassurance. I encouraged them by saying, "I will show you how to overcome adversity. I will show you how to endure pain and still keep your composure and do what's right no matter what." Even if no one else understands and you don't know all the details, you must know in your heart that you did the right thing. People are watching you. They are depending upon you to get back up. This is why I want my book to give hope, and encouragement that there is life after divorce. Everything you endured in one season is preparation for restoration in the next.

"Instead of your shame, there shall be a double portion; instead of dishonor they shall rejoice in their lot; therefore, in their land they shall possess a double portion; they shall have everlasting joy" (Isaiah 61:7, NASB).

A Second Chance

Yet this I call to mind and therefore I have hope: Because of the LORD's great love we are not consumed, for his compassions never fail. They are new every morning; great is your faithfulness.
Lamentations 3:21-23, NIV

A second chance is a blessing. It's another chance to try again. And another opportunity to redeem yourself from a past mistake or failure. Getting a second chance in the aftermath of a divorce is especially gracious. There are many people who never reach emotional restoration after being deeply wounded from an acrimonious split. As for me, I never imagined I would end up being divorced. My parents were a model for an enduring marriage. They never divorced, and it was my testimony that no matter what, I'd never get divorced either. When you're standing at the altar saying "I do," you can't imagine ending up in divorce court under irreconcilable differences. In a perfect world, divorce wouldn't happen, but they do. When it does you have to keep a positive attitude. It's not the end of the world. Above all, have faith in God, that He will see you through. One thing is for sure, He'll never leave or forsake you. Let God work. Let Him redeem time for you. When He redeems time, He is giving you that blessed second chance. A chance to recover, to restore and live again.

No one wants to experience difficulty. An age-old question is, Why do bad things happen to good people? No one wants their spouse to get sick, or their children to get hurt. You don't want to slip and fall down the stairs or be involved in a traffic accident. You don't want any of that. But life is going to happen regardless. You can't stop moving forward for fear of facing trials and adversity. Especially, when you are the cause of the problem you must learn from it, to become a better version of yourself. The key is, once God has given you a second chance, you must give yourself a second chance as well. God allows you to start over again with that second chance. Therefore, utilize the lessons you learned so you won't make the same mistake twice.

I've learned to appreciate even the uncomfortable circumstances of my life, because in those circumstances God was working out His plan. All things that we face may not be good, but God can work them out for the good! The Lord knew there was a better position, a better place, and a better person for me. However, in order for me to get to my preferred place, would have never happen unless I had passed through the valley of divorce. Yes, it was painful. However, I had to look at the bright side of it, by finding the good in my situation. I had to focus on the light at the end of the tunnel in order to find my way out.

You may ask yourself, what good can come out of a divorce? I asked the same question. That's when God began to reveal this to me. One of the good things that came out of my previous marriage is that I have over twenty years of experience. Experience is very helpful. Learning how to live with and love another individual takes a lot of patience and understanding. Learning how to compromise and appreciate someone else's feelings and point of view is key in maintaining a dynamic relationship. Great marriages do not just happen by themselves. They take work. It's not just about you; your desires, or your feelings.

Now I know what helps me. I know what marriage is. I know what being a good husband is. I know what it means to be married and what it takes. You have to pull from that experience and learn from your mistakes so love and marriage can work, even when it's the second time around.

Day 2

DEALING WITH NEGATIVE THOUGHTS

When I am afraid, I put my trust in you.
Psalm 56:3, NIV

When you're in dark places, you deal with a lot of negative thoughts. The most persistent negative thought that I wrestled with was that I was a failure. I felt that I would never overcome the stigma of being a divorcee. Stigmas stagnate you. They keep you stuck in the past and discourage forward progress. I reached a point where couldn't bear the thought of being in love and married again. I was still recovering from divorce trauma. I wasn't in any shape to reengage in a relationship. I was just trying to get myself together.

All at once, life presented a perfect storm. I was going through a divorce. I caught COVID-19 then pneumonia which brought on a number of secondary health challenges. To top that off, I stayed with my brother for a few months to quarantine from COVID. After that, I moved back in with my mother. Imagine, getting a divorce, going through COVID, then having to move back home with my mother. It was tough.

In the midst of me going through such difficult times, a lot of bad thoughts went through my mind. I wanted to hurt myself. I wanted to hurt others. In this world you are always taught a man is supposed to be strong who can confront tough situations and tough it out. However, that was not my reality. My self-esteem was low, and my confidence was nonexistent. I was depressed and didn't feel good about myself, because I was carrying too much stress. But I had to learn to endure, because giving up was not an option. That's a key point. Be sure to endure by holding on to your faith.

It is amazing how things can get so gloomy and dark where not even an inkling of light seeps through. At this point you must turn to God who is the true light, so that He can be a lamp unto your feet and a light unto your path. He is the one who can help you keep a level head so that the situation won't knock you out for the count. Always keep in mind strong individuals can take a beating and through the Lord's help, get back up again. Stumbling will happen. You may have the scars to show for it. However, when you stand up that gives you another opportunity to be a testimony of what the Lord can do even when you have been through the darkness of divorce. That's why never give up on yourself, because there is a testimony in it for somebody else that will go through what you came out of.

Never let your mind tell you things are over just because situations don't go the way you like. Sometimes you just have to reset yourself in order to see it another way. Just remain faithful and focused because there are multiple ways your circumstances can play out. Many times, I blamed myself. It's like self-imposed darkness. This dark place is where it keeps you so negative that nothing seems to be positive. Nothing cheers you up. That's when you become one of those angry negative people that no one wants to be around. This is not a good place for anyone to be. It's like traveling through an endless tunnel where you are ever moving and never stopping to rest. The questions is How do you get out? Excellent question. First your mind has to be made up that you want better for your life. The fact that you have to make your mind up to get out is a significant thing because that means you have not embraced these bad circumstances as your new normal. When you decide that you want to make that first step towards the light, your heart has made the shift that creates a pathway to your healing and deliverance.

Good can often come out of bad times and these low places in life. Being in those places can uncover something deep inside you never knew you had. We all have the power to change our circumstances therefore, we also have the power to change the circumstances around us. Each one of us has this "powerful place" within us. Sometimes it takes a bad situation to unlock our powerful place. Life is hard, but hard is needed to navigate to your place of strength. But first you must gather yourself to calculate the next move. In sports, offensive and defensive tactics are drawn up in order to defeat the opposing team. It is the same way in life. You must employ a winning strategy, by consulting with God and His word in order to defeat the enemies in your life. The winner and champion part of me has always been there. But by going through this dark place, I never knew I had this in me. Yes, all things worked together for my good so God could get all the glory. During my dark times I couldn't see the blissful times I'm experiencing right now. That is why you never give up. No matter how many times you fall, stay in the race.

Don't get caught up with the mess you made because it will get better. Push through the mess to obtain the manifestation from God. Don't walk around in a woe is me, victims' mentality. People don't have to know what you're going through just by looking at you. Clean yourself up. Stay fresh clean and smelling good. Even while you're going through keep walking in victory. You are preparing for your future happy place, so get ready. Start confessing that favor is on your life. You're more than a conqueror and you will succeed in life.

Some people really don't know how powerful they are. When life throws you an upper cut it hits hard. However, shake it off and counter-punch. Stay in the ring and continue to fight back. The battle is not given to the swift, nor to the strong, but to those who endure to the end. So, when the past comes to mind, you must disengage those thoughts, so you won't get stuck there. Pull down those strongholds and every high thought that exalts itself against the knowledge of God. Believe and confess what God has already declared about you. You are a winner and more than a conqueror.

Review your past and take all the good from it but leave the negative parts there. You have to segregate the negative from the positive. When your past experiences come back as a trigger acknowledge it but move past. These instances can be a hindrance or a blessing in disguise. Why do we look at bad things and just think about all the contrary stuff that accompanies it. We must acknowledge that nothing that comes our way is a surprise to God. He already knows how to deliver you from whatever you're facing. Magnify the Lord not the negative circumstances. We spend so much time blowing up the bad and forget about blowing up the goodness of God.

There are many things that will confront you in life, that are not all your fault. Much of what we deal with on a daily basis is beyond our control. However, it is important to take ownership of your own mistakes, so you can grow from it. It is important to think through problems with a clear perspective. Once negativity gets you down it can hold you hostage. People have a tendency to think the worst about our circumstances. However, that's just in your mind. Many of these things never come to pass. This is a dangerous spot to be in because it can cause you to make the wrong decision or make a bad choice. This is why the Bible says, "…whatever is true, whatever is honorable, whatever is right, whatever is pure, whatever is lovely, whatever is of good repute, if there is any excellence and if anything, worthy of praise, dwell on these things (Phil. 4:8, NASB).

Your past should only be a quick reminder of how far you have come! Indeed, what I had to go through years ago was a setup for my blissful season now. The chaos I was going through was simply a prerequisite for my blessing. The obstacles I encountered were upward steps to a higher level. That's where I found my place of increase. A quick tip is when negative thoughts come, don't let them stay. You can't stop a bird from flying over your head, but you can stop them from landing and building a nest. Never settle for a cloud of uncertainty when there is a bright future ahead of you. GOD will guide you to a bright and beautiful future.

Time passes by so quickly when you are focused on the wrong things, which amounts to wasting your time. Negative thinking has a way of clouding your vision. Dark spots cover up what is hopeful and good. When I was in the dark spots, I never thought that I would see the light of joy and liberty. Now I'm in a pleasant place and it not only feels good, but it is good. Life is hard enough, don't let the wrong person into your life to contribute to it. This is why the Bible declares, "*Whoso* findeth a wife findeth a good *thing*, and obtaineth favour of the LORD (Proverbs 18:22, KJV). Yes, love is so important these days that when you know what you have, it's truly a gift, so please treasure it.

Day 3

OVERCOMING THE DARK PLACES

For His anger is but for a moment, His favor is for life; Weeping may endure for a night, But joy comes in the morning.
Psalm 30:5, NKJV

Therapy helped me get through my divorce. Going to church helped me keep the faith. However, going back to church was tough at times. When you have been in a church for years and people know you, every time they see you, they ask, "Where's your wife?" Every single Sunday I had to replay, "Where is your wife?" and every single Sunday I had to replay, "We're going through divorce, so we're not together."

These moments felt like quicksand. In order to keep your sanity, you have to understand your *why*. Why are you here? You must understand that God has a purpose for you though you may not see the purpose while going through the turmoil. You're trying to get out but not making much headway. It's like trying to walk up a down escalator. You take one step forward but regardless; it just keeps pulling you back down. You have to acknowledge, yes, it's difficult. However, this is not the first trial that you have been through. You already know that this too shall come to pass. Though it seems like we may be all alone when we are going through, we're not. People go through similar or worse every day. Don't let those negative thoughts isolate you, as if you're the only one in the world with problems. Everyone has something to deal with. Even Jesus!

A good weapon to fight against depression and shame was to learn how to be thankful in whatever situation I was going through. When I was in the hospital, I didn't have to make it out. Let that be said! When I was dealing with COVID and pneumonia, I would hear on the news how many people were dying each day. I understood that many didn't make it out that same situation, but GOD upheld and delivered me. My hope was only in Jesus. That's why you have to have a firm foundation of who you believe in. I kept thinking about my kids going through the situation and wanting to be an example to them. And I realized that if I fail, if I don't do anything else with my life, it means I didn't glorify God. Ultimately, he has to get the glory. I looked back at Job and all that he went through. I thought, "If Job could go through what he went through, then I know I can get through this." I learned to encourage myself in the LORD.

So the blissfulness you see me with today is a result of coming through a very dark spot in my life. It was like being trapped in a room with no light only trying to think positive that everything will work out. Being in this spot requires patience and perseverance just to think that it will be okay. Being patient is key because it takes time mentally to get you through. You have to process situations that have led you to this point. For me it was patience plus forgiveness of myself to get the breakthrough I needed. Forgiveness is so vital to your healing when coming out of a dark spot knowing you have something to do with it. Just admit the wrong that was done in order to move forward with your life.

As a man, I had so much tension and stress built up in me that I had to see a therapist. It was the best thing I did that helped me during these difficult times. There's nothing wrong with seeing a therapist because they have gone to school and are skilled in helping you navigate through these deep emotional and psychological issues. I had to forgive myself and the ones that were affected by these issues and then seek the assistance to help me make a full recovery. Your conscience can be so clogged with second guessing yourself. If I had only not let it get this far. If I had only seen this coming, etc. So when you second guess yourself you have all these questions looping nonstop through your brain, it can drive you crazy. That's why it's necessary to seek help from wise counsel.

Don't worry about what people say about going to therapy. The truth be told, the same ones talking are in need of therapy just like you. Someone else's opinion about you can stop your destiny, if you let it interfere with your plans. Everyone has an opinion, but they are not the ones walking in your shoes. The key is to be true to yourself and stop telling people your business. A lot of what they are saying is in response to what you told them. Also, never let someone dictate how you think about something. It's okay to hear someone out about a matter then decide how you want to proceed with that suggestion. If you feel a certain way about it, then go with your gut feeling. I felt so destitute in my situation that I had to get help for my mental state. That's why I encourage people to see a therapist after your life is turned upside down. I didn't see how I could get back on my feet. Yes, I believe in God. I know he can make a way. At this moment your trust has to be so strong that faith comes over you so mightily.

As people, we are very sensitive. At times it seems like we feel so much that it exacerbates our pain. But remember there is light at the end of the tunnel. I know it's easier said than done but trust me I'm a living witness. If it happened for me, it could happen for you. We have all heard that saying that things happen for a reason. Well, I didn't understand it at first but, this situation happened in my life so I could be better, stronger, and wiser than before. That's why I said even in your dark spots always remember that life will get better. Do not allow negativity and darkness to blot out the light that's coming your way.

Be Open to Receive Someone

Do not conform to the pattern of this world, but be transformed by the renewing of your mind. Then you will be able to test and approve what God's will is— his good, pleasing and perfect will.
Romans 12:2, NIV

If you truly desire to have someone in your life, you have to be open because everyone is different. If you plan on getting married, then you have to realize that you're going to be spending the rest of your life with another individual. A couple is two different personalities. They do and say things differently. They may get on your nerves, but you have to be able to understand and get along with that person. It's about knowing and understanding each other.

People are quick to get into a relationship, but you need to know and understand the other person. You need to understand where they came from. You need to get to know their family. Go around that family and see if it's what you want.

Everybody has that crazy someone in the family. I've got a lot of them. But if the whole family is crazy, then you might not need to get involved with them because that's a big red flag from up front. The red flags are another thing. Everybody has issues, but when you start seeing red flags on the first date, the second time, then the third time, that's pretty much a strikeout!

Nobody will tell you everything about them up front. However, whatever they are trying to hide, it will eventually come to the light. Their actions will show you who they really are. You need to be a judge of good character and be careful of who you are associating with. When I saw a red flag from the start, it was a one-time date. We'd go out to eat and that's it. They were not getting another call because that would be allowing the wrong person into my life. Don't let them get a foothold, because the next thing you know, you're dealing with the whole boatload. Then your whole life will become complicated and compromised.

Taking a chance on love is simply having faith beyond what you feel. Not only can you have love, it can be demonstrated so profoundly in your world. I get it. It may be tough because I had been hurt before. Overcoming to get where I am today was very difficult. Going through the hardest times in my life but had an inclination that it could all be over any day. I could only think that I have to keep going through the dark to get to the light. How you perceive something is how it will look in the future. In other words, have so much faith in God's plan for your life that doubt has no chance.

Getting this type of tenacity will place fear in a headlock. Be bold about your newfound assurance and your relationship shall work. The more poise you possess your whole body takes formation to new depths. Having such fortitude radiates strength, so keep walking tall and strong. This feeling is like nothing else in the world. Whatever you put your hands to do will be great. If you are suffering from defeat, I was once in your shoes and felt I could never be great. However, through letting God guide me and therapy, I am a much better man with a healthy self-esteem and confidence. The lessons made me who I am today.

It just seemed like life happened all over again for me. It's been a fantastic journey thus far. So, a man really knows when he found the one, it's a fact. I'm a living witness because I knew Sophia was the one for me within two weeks of just talking on the phone. I can say that because our conversations covered everything from childhood talk, church talk, life situations etc. As the days went by it's like we just belonged together. I wanted to let her know I was a serious man and that I genuinely cared for her. I had to let her know that she was the one for me. That's when the contemplating and the planning started. When you are serious about a woman, the right thing to do is to put a ring on her finger. Making that decision caused me to take action. When should I propose? Where should I propose? What type of ring should I get? Those questions and more.

So, at this point in my life, I realize that this is where my life should be. God will surely see you through when you put him first. June 11, 2022, was our first day talking on the phone. It was amazing. We really enjoyed each other. It was as if we had known each other for a long time. To have someone in your life that really understands and appreciates you is priceless. Sophia has shown me love from the beginning of our friendship to now. It really was blissful just getting to know each other.

While Sophia and I were talking on the phone, a thought came to me. "She's my missing piece." Like an incomplete puzzle, Sophia was the piece that was so hard to find. Once I found that piece it brought me so much joy. Finally, I was able to say "yes" she's the one. Now the picture is complete. It was such a relief when Sophia entered my life. The divorce left me wounded and heartbroken. Sophia's love was like a healing balm whose love and tenderness mended my broken heart. So yes, it's true, God is able to do exceedingly abundantly above all that you could ask or think! I realized that Sophia coming into my life was the best thing that could happen to me. Now I feel whole again. Now I can love and trust again.

A year and a half ago, I would not have believed that I was on the path to being married again. It's only by the grace of God that has brought me to this beautiful place in my life. Just to think that I have found my partner for the rest of my life is so precious to me. I never saw myself wanting to say "I do" again if it wasn't going to be right. However, Sophia's love persuaded me. The second time around, I've never been in love like this before. I tell her all the time that I love her. Love is multifaceted and dynamic requiring action and demonstration, not just words. With each passing day, I am eager to show her how much I love her. I fall in love with her each and every day.

From the first week of talking to Sophia on the phone I knew something was totally different. This was no ordinary superficial feeling. The reason I say that is because when you deeply love someone and they love you back, it's enough to keep you going. To give you a new perspective on life. Going above and beyond for the one you love is quite gratifying. You want to be good to them. You want to show them how much you care. There is an inner peace and a conformation in your spirit about them. So, when you know that you have found your soulmate it is indescribable. You want to be near them. You start missing them even though you saw them five minutes ago. I know I'm making a fuss, but this is just how I feel about my Sophia. I'm blessed and I'm proud to tell the world about it.

Day 5

DON'T ATTEMPT TO DUPLICATE WHAT SOMEONE ELSE HAS

and to put on the new self, created to be like God in true righteousness and holiness.
Ephesians 4:24, NIV

Everyone is unique. We all have different strengths, weaknesses, abilities, gifts and talents. We also have a unique way using our abilities to reach desired outcomes and goals. Just because a person accomplishes something one way, does not mean that someone else can do it the way they did it. What someone else has, or what someone else does may not be something the casual observer may be able to duplicate. Even though you may be inspired by that person, you have to realize that's them, not you. Trying to be someone you are not will lead to frustration and failure. Try specializing in being the best you. No one is better at being you—than you.

Trying to duplicate what someone else has done is like you're trying to reap where someone else has sown. You can't reap someone else's harvest. For example, I like LeBron James. No one else in the league has played that long. The reason why is because he spends almost one to two million dollars on his body. There's no way you could even try to say that you can reap at the same level as him and for as long as he has. Even if you did put in the work, or spent the money, or used the same exercise regimen, there's only one LeBron. You will not get the same result because he is unique and so are you.

You can't reap what someone else has sown. It's like wanting to collect rent income on a rental property that you do not own. That doesn't make sense. You cannot benefit from someone else's hard work and success like that. That's why we need to seek God for His purpose for our lives so that we don't waste time try to duplicate something that is not designed for us. Our blessings are designed specifically for us. I say for us, because of what Sophia and I have now. What Sophia went through last year before meeting me, and what I went through as she was going through, that was God designing our blessing for us. And since God designed it for us, it's working out for our good.

God was putting it all together and realizing that Tommy and Sophia would make a great couple. They can do great things together because they are two different people and two different personalities. We can learn from each other, which is a good thing because in marriage you're supposed to bring out the best in each other. He knew that there was something inside of me, like this book *Later Date*. I didn't know. I didn't have a clue. But God knew that Sophia has written books and has expertise in this area. The Bible declares, "He who finds a wife finds a good thing And obtains favor from the LORD (Proverbs 18:22, NASB). So now I'm obtaining the Lord's favor by writing this book. Sophia is already a successful author. Consulting with her about my book project has opened up a new path for ministry and success. I can only imagine all the good things that will come from our marriage. The favor of God is in what we have together.

It is important not to let the wrong people have influence over you. There will be many important decisions you will have to make, some of them life changing. If you let them, people will try to tell you how to propose. They will try to give their opinion on how to plan the wedding. Others will try to get into every aspect of your business and advise you on every detail. However, I obtained wise counsel on every aspect of our wedding. If you don't know something, ask somebody, but make sure it's the right somebody. What I did was I sought out wise counsel. I received the blessing from the people I knew were godly examples and people of character and standards. I wasn't concerned about impressing anyone. I only wanted to make God happy, Sophia happy, and make her dad, Apostle John, and my Bishop E. L. Usher happy. That's it. I had to honor the right people. When you honor the right people, and you do things the way you're supposed to, you can expect to reap a blessing from God.

I am still amazed that over 114,000 people viewed our wedding. In an instant I was catapulted onto a very large stage.

Little ole me! This is totally new to me. Sophia was already popular. She has a large social media following. Her conferences are well attended. But to a great extent I now share in her celebrity. I'm by her side practically everywhere she goes. I didn't see myself as ever being in the so-called limelight, but God did. It was a fairy tale wedding and a whirlwind marriage. These last few months I have traveled more than I ever have. It's been amazing. I just give praise to God.

Let me encourage you to seek God for direction for your life. He knows the plans that he has for you. Don't look for people to give you directions. Don't look to social media for the latest advice and trends. Don't try to keep up with the Joneses but be diligent and seek God for yourself. Other people's opinions won't pay your bills or buy your clothes. They're not going to buy you a house. You have to take charge of your own affairs. Don't build on another person's foundation. With the Lord's help, you can build a great life on your own foundation.

Day 6

THE DIFFERENCE BETWEEN NEED AND WANT

And this is my prayer: that your love may abound more and more in know ledge and depth of insight
Philippians 1:9, NIV

There's a big difference between what you need and what you want. A need is a necessity, something that you must have to make the days go by. In a relationship, you need someone who's going to love you for who you are and treat you the way you want to be treated. On the other hand, a want is something that you really desire. For example, you may want someone to be or look a certain type of way. There is nothing wrong with having desires for both needs and wants. That's what makes a successful relationship. When you know the difference between the two, it helps you understand what to expect from the relationship.

Needs can be so deeply embedded in our heart that it takes God to help realize that they are there. For example, a person may have been emotionally wounded as a child. They need deliverance, but what they think they want is drugs and alcohol to mask the pain. However, a need is something that's going to help you improve and elevate you to the next level. On my path to wholeness, my therapist asked me to write out my needs and wants. I didn't realize the impact this would have on my life. I saw this as nothing more than a simple writing assignment. But this was actually a very powerful tool to unlock some great potential for my future, especially when I began a relationship with Sophia. After learning about how cathartic and liberating it was for her to write about her former life and transformation, now I understand why I needed to write about my journey. While I was writing, I was also releasing. Every moment I had I would be writing down thoughts, feelings, and insights on my phone. I wasn't writing just to be writing, but it was for this book. Truly, God knew what I needed. He placed Sophia in my life for a reason. I had already started the book, but I needed her to push *Later Date* out of me.

Now let's deal with the *want* side of things. I wanted to have someone to love me for who I am and accept me for the person I was becoming. It is difficult to adapt to someone else's perception of who they think you should be. Under that scenario, you are always adjusting but never satisfying yourself or the other person. This is why understanding the difference between *a need* and *a want* is so important. When you really take time to understand the place that needs and wants to have in your life, then you are in a better position to take charge and benefit from a loving relationship.

When you fall to low points in your life, you discover things about yourself that you may not have realized before. There will be some good and bad things that must be dealt with. But regardless of what you discover, it is important to remain positive. We fail to realize that pain can play an important part in our deliverance. These situations can be your most critical moments to gain power and understand how to navigate to better times. Bad experiences can be turned around for better outcomes in your life. I'm sure you have heard the saying, "if life brings you lemons, then make lemonade." Work through your situations. How life turns out is often the result of how you respond to its circumstances. Staying focused on the right goals determines where you end up. This is why having a positive outlook on life is so important. It's not only a matter of positive thinking, but it's all about trusting God to lead and guide you into all truth and being ready to take action when the time is right.

Beautiful things are often the result of coming up through adverse circumstances. Take the rose for example, its colors are so beautiful, but it did not begin that way. All that beauty came from a not so beautiful beginning from a little seedling that looked nothing like the rose. It was out of sight and buried in dirt. However, it had a purpose. Greatness was already programmed into the seed. The rose didn't say I'm going to stay in the ground. No, it said, I need light. Therefore, it kept growing until it broke through the ground. Once it got its breakthrough, it could fully bloom. Like the rose, you too must keep pressing towards your breakthrough, because there is an astonishing future ahead for you. After the rose breaks through the dirt, now the dirt nourishes and supports the rose. That's the turnaround, where God makes even the bad things work out for your good. The pain, tribulation, dissatisfaction, and worries are all setting up for a powerful comeback. It is possible that the life you *want*, just *needed* some nourishing, so you could blossom into the person God would have you to be.

Day 7

DATING FOR COMPANIONSHIP

One who has unreliable friends soon comes to ruin, but there is a friend who sticks closer than a brother.
Proverbs 18:24, NIV

After my divorce was final, there was a void in my life. To fill this void, I started dating for a season. I wasn't trying to find a new wife. But I did desire to have some companionship. After twenty years of marriage, being single and lonely was a strange place for me to be. An intense committed relationship is not what I was looking for. I just didn't want to be lonely. However, I needed to get myself right first. I was still on the rebound. My emotional state hadn't quite recovered. I wanted friendship and I wanted to take it slow. From my perspective I was not looking to overwhelm whomever I was dating by spoiling them right away. I just wanted to have fun, go out to the movies, eat, and that's it. No strings attached. There were women who knew I was recently divorced and showed interest in me, but

I was not interested in them. If I pursued anyone it would have to be on my terms, not theirs.

Looking back at it now, dating was not the right direction for me to be going. In fact, dating turned out to be more of a distraction. In a sense it was my way to self-medicate. I was trying to find relief. But I soon discovered that dating could not return me to wholeness. It wasn't a faster way for me to restore my mental health. In dating you're focused on impressing the other person. All along, my priority should have been to get myself right. It was important to be right within myself because if you're not right mentally, then you are in no shape for the challenges of a relationship. At this stage of life, being in my mid-forties, it was traumatizing when our marriage of twenty years came to a sudden end. In the aftermath of our divorce, I was feeling like a failure. My self-esteem and confidence in myself was nonexistent. For a long time, I didn't wish to socially engage. My life primarily consisted of going to work and occasionally going out on the weekend. Mainly I just stayed home.

After all that I had been through, then I got sick with COVID. This virus took a toll on me mentally and physically because I had a fairly severe case. So, by the time I started dating I had just come out of a whirlwind of physical and emotional issues. Therefore, dating became taxing quickly. It wasn't exciting but it became boring. It wasn't long after that I came to my senses and realized that a date can't help me. I just wanted to live right, so I said to the Lord, "I'm just tired but I don't want to waste my time and displease you." I wanted companionship because I was familiar with that. I know what marriage is like and I wanted it again. It was at that point when I told God I really wanted to remarry. After that, everything happened so fast. I reached out to First Lady Tawanda Usher, and she said, "You know, see what Sophia's doing." And the rest is history. From our first conversation it really touched my heart and that loneliness started to fade. I just thank God that it happened the way that it did.

Being in love with someone who really loves you back is so essential. This type of dynamic relationship is what's required for lasting happiness. Just saying "I do" is not enough to keep a couple together. True love is action not just talk. Action is so important in relationships because it demonstrates and causes forward motion. Then your partner can gage the progress by your actions. That's when you're doing necessary things to have a successful relationship. Growing together is very important because it allows things to change for the better for each other while your relationship matures.

Day 8

WHEN A MAN KNOWS, HE KNOWS

*Do not be anxious about anything, but in every situation,
by prayer and petition, with thanksgiving,
present your requests to God.
Philippians 4:6, NIV*

A man knows in his heart who he wants to be with. It's something that you feel every time you see them, and you're around them. Even when you're not around them, you're still thinking about them. If you're with someone but you're thinking about someone else, then she's probably not that one you want to spend the rest of your life with. You should be thinking only about that individual. I'm not saying that you don't think about anything else, just not *someone* else. It's a feeling inside and you just know.

When I first started talking to Sophia on the phone, I knew there was something special. It wasn't because of who she was. It wasn't because of her popularity. It was the genuine conversations that we had. We talked about real life matters. We had heart-to-heart conversations. We were honest and vulnerable with each other. Nothing was off the table. From there, our feelings for each other began to grow and a deeper connection began to develop. Honesty and trust is the necessary environment for love to grow. That's when your heart starts to skip a beat when you're around that person. That stuff is real because I experienced it for myself. Even when we exchanged text messages, the emotional response was the same. It's so special to know when you have someone to talk to that knows what you've been through and understands you.

Now that we are married, I am often asked, how did you know Sophia was the one? Let me answer that this way. Imagine everything just being right on point. Where all the pieces fall into place. I would describe it as amazed, stunned, and astonished. It's like the bliss of a fairytale love story that's intriguing and magical. Yes indeed, love like this really exists. This feeling is so worth fighting for and putting your past behind you. The joy you get by being with someone who truly loves you is so special. It's like being overwhelmed with passion, that something so wonderful could happen to me. Knowing that you have obtained such favor from the Lord, when for so long you didn't feel like you deserve another chance at love. This excitement should be felt all over the world. Knowing that two people fell in love so effortlessly, should be headline news.

It Doesn't Take Years

*I thought, 'Age should speak; advanced
years should teach wisdom.'*
Job 32:7, NIV

How long does it take to know you have found the right one? The answers can vary. Some would say at least a couple years. Others would be more aggressive and respond for a year or several months. However, in our case it was even sooner than that. It all has to do with the couple and their mindset. In my case I was tired of playing games. I asked the Lord for what I needed and wanted, and He gave me exactly what I asked for. Therefore, I believe people can know right away. The difference is that some people don't recognize the signs. There is a deeper sense that will be in agreement with what you are experiencing from that person. When things line up, you can move forward. When you make that connection, the togetherness begins to work. You should never try to force it, or go against what your heart is telling you. A dishonest person will wear a facade of honesty. However, when their words and actions do not agree, that cannot be ignored. In most cases the truth is staring us right in the face.

It is important that you understand what it is that I'm saying. It didn't take long for Sophia and me, but I acknowledge that every case is different. Since marriage is a lifelong commitment, you should take as much time as needed. However, having said that, I am against people wasting time in dead end relationships that are going nowhere. Though each couple's timeline may be different, none of us have time, energy, and effort to waste. That's what I am saying, brothers, don't waste hers or your time.

A man knows when he has found the right woman. He has to come to a place where he stops playing around. Many men want to procrastinate because they are afraid of being in a committed relationship. Even when they know the woman they have found is the best thing for them, they keep putting it off because they are insecure and are used to putting things off. However, that's not the woman's fault, that's your set of issues that have always kept you from moving forward in relationships. But there is one thing you have to understand, we all have a limited amount of time on this earth, and the clock is ticking. These years go by quickly. If you find a piece of gold, you don't have to waste time wondering if it is real or not. Take it, refine it, and make something beautiful out of it.

June 24, 2022, is a special day that I will never forget. I consider it as my unofficial anniversary date. That's the day I discovered what love felt like again. To have someone in my life who put a smile on my face, who made me laugh and experience joy again, was simply marvelous. This is a joy that I wish everyone could experience. With that much love going forth I believe the world would change for the better.

More Than Just a Date

The LORD set a time and said, "Tomorrow the LORD will do this in the land."
Exodus 9:5, NIV

I knew it was more than just a date when I looked across the table and saw the happiness in Sophia's eyes. It was just a great feeling to be around her and go out on a date. I was just in awe of her, especially when I would attend one of her speaking engagements and watch her preach. It was amazing to see her going forth in ministry and seeing God using her in such a powerful way. Then after seeing her preach was one thing, but then in the natural being on a date with her was an additional blessing. People often forget that God may use a person in a powerful way, but they are still people with natural needs. I'm so glad that I am part of her natural too. That really puts a smile on my face, and makes my liver quiver! God gave me a prophet and a good woman too. Praise God! Now I'm walking in thankfulness and gratefulness. Even though I had come through darkness to a glorious situation like this. To have such peace of mind and to feel love again, always amazes me.

So, as I reflect back to the first date, when I held her hands as we blessed our food, I just knew God was doing something great. By the end of the meal as we were boxing up the food, I just knew this was the beginning of something bigger and better. Sophia was the one. After we had eaten, holding her hand and gazing into her lovely eyes, I felt love like I had never felt it before.

If you're inspired by my story and thinking, "I want that. How do I get that too?" My take is you can have it. You can have love too. First, you have to truly believe that you deserve everything that you desire, everything that you want, and how you want it. Life is about making it happen. Also, it's about letting God be in it to make it happen for you. The foundation is the key. Get your foundation right first. As the Bible declares, know that God is in it, and that He will supply all your needs according to His riches in glory. Even when you're going through despair and it seems like it'll never get right, I'm a true believer that God can do greater than what you can even ask or think. But it is according to the power that works within you. Take my word for it. God is truly able.

I would have never thought it possible that I could get back on my feet in my forties. It's just a true miracle of what I've been through in going from owning two homes, to not having a place of my own to stay. You only have to believe. That's all you can do. When you put your belief and your faith in God, I guarantee that everything you think, want, desire, and dream can come to pass.

Building a strong friendship with Sophia was my priority. It is important how the relationship started because that provides the context for moving forward. I felt as though this new friendship could be something extraordinary. My plans were to take it one day at a time and get to know Sophia. Not try to rush anything, but to let nature take its course. From the beginning we had an open dialogue. I wasn't trying to hide anything, and neither was she. This was refreshing because normally when you start dating the point is to hide the past. However, this was not the path that we took. I had a past and needed to tell all, and so did she. I'm not ashamed of my past because it actually made me the man that's writing this book now. Little did I know that my gloomy days would open up to luminous days. We have truly been blessed. Starting out as true friends led to her becoming my fiancé, to my bride, and now to my wife. Each step was worth taking.

Day 11

THE LATER DATE CONTINUES

In this way they will lay up treasure for themselves as a firm foundation for the coming age, so that they may take hold of the life that is truly life.
1 Timothy 6:19, NIV

You may ask, what is the significance to the title of the book, "later date?" It was something I said to Sophia in one of our early conversations over the phone. It was completely off the cuff, but it had a nice ring to it. However, later on God told me it would be the title of a book where I would share snippets of my story to encourage and be a blessing to others.

Later Date is about having something good that sparks expectation and hope. It's something that's happening at a later time, an opportune time. It's an ongoing anticipation that brings gladness about the coming of a brighter day. Before I married Sophia, later date was the proposal, then later date was the marriage. Later date was the anticipation and expectation that something next was pending. Later date was taking trips together. Later date is going with her when she's preaching, vacationing and social activities. Later date is a life of growing together and getting to know each other. Later date is going to the grocery store, cooking dinner together, watching movies, and building a future together. Later date is an ongoing journey. It will always be an ongoing thing because my wife and I are still dating. Later date is a forever honeymoon. So, later date entails a lot of things, it's simply having fun together and enjoying life together.

Later date is a blissful feeling. It was a whirlwind of emotions that have led up to now. I'm just so thankful I didn't stay stuck in my darkest days. The enemy wanted me to quit because he knew the destiny that was coming forth out of me. The blessings that were on the way.

Let me encourage you. God has tailor made blessings designed specifically for you, because the trials and your tribulations you came out of, were specially designed to shape you. We have to remember that we are on the potter's wheel. God shapes us into the vessel he purposed us to be. While we are going through that divine shaping process, we experience difficulty and pain. The enemy wanted you to give up. But it will not be so! I'm so glad you are reading this book because there is a later date bliss waiting for you. There's always a reason to keep going because your destiny is waiting for you to arrive. The trials and tribulations you have gone through do not define you, but come to shape you. God uses these things, though they are not good, to take you to the place that he has called you. Just because you cried and even feel like staying in bed seems like nothing is going right, is the very reason why you should keep trusting God. It takes both negative and positive current for any electronic device to work. Going through the negative to get to your positive is often how things come to pass.

How to Experience Later Date

Continue your love to those who know you, your righteousness to the upright in heart.
Psalm 36:10, NIV

If you want to experience *later date* you must know what you want. But first, make sure you're ready. Make sure your heart and mind are ready and that you're open to receiving someone. It's not a matter of just saying, "Oh, okay. I want someone now." No, you need to be ready. You need to write down the things that you want and desire. Write down the characteristics you would like. Be precise and purposeful. If you fail to do so, then one day you might end up with what you weren't hoping for.

God wants to give you what you truly desire. He doesn't randomly say, "Oh, I'm going to give you this person." No, he wants to give you someone that you enjoy being with, that you don't mind waking up to every single morning. You don't mind going with them to the grocery store. You don't mind taking them places, doing things for them, or having fun together. Write down what you really want and then make sure you're truly open to receiving someone. Make sure your past relationship is not holding you back, that you're not bringing in baggage from the past. One of the key factors in getting over someone who hurt you is you forgiving them. That's what allows you to move on.

What makes a good couple stay together? Well, it's a lot of factors that can be considered in this question. Having God in your life is first and foremost. If we seek the kingdom of God and his righteousness, the things will be added. God knows what you need before you ask Him. Acknowledge Him in all your ways and he will direct your paths. What we desire, what we obtain, how we maneuver, and everything in between will only come as a result of the Lord. This is the foundation that must be established to build a great relationship.

Communication is definitely important to have on both sides. It has to be a togetherness for dialogue so you can understand from another point of view. Just talking through certain situations in life is therapeutic to really understand moments in life. Sometimes you just may need to be the listening ear so your mate can just vent their feelings. Life's pressures affect us all. We all have those difficult days where you just need to get things off your chest. So that's why in a relationship both parties should talk about how their day was to each other. It is also important to be considerate of the other person and really listen to them. Be respectful of feelings and emotions, because we are not the same. Always keep in mind that we process things differently. There will always be the other side of the coin to consider.

Trustworthiness is so important to a great relationship. Trust is key from the beginning and throughout your journey of love. Being intentional in life is a must for a satisfying relationship. Going the extra mile is an extremely valuable thing to do because it shows that you don't mind spending the necessary effort to make things work. Paying attention to detail and understanding how your mate thinks is important in getting along. You have to study your mate to know what they like and don't like. Learning their personality is very crucial in obtaining more insight about your mate.

Being compassionate to your mate is a must, it helps you discern situations. Day by day we should get closer to our mates, that way you can feel each other without even saying anything. This ability is a way to connect on another level that will last a lifetime. Understanding is one more key ingredient to a successful relationship. It's simple to do, however some mishandle this concept resulting in disappointment or disagreement. Avoiding such things is vital for a flourishing relationship that can pass the test of time. Being appreciative to your mate will keep them feeling good about themselves. Staying positive with each other and keeping a good mindset about life will definitely enhance the journey of love. Make sure to stay grateful for your mate, this helps you realize how much they mean to you every second of the day. Be supportive of your mate because at the end of the day you must have each other's back.

Being affectionate keeps love flowing through you to your mate. Stay devoted to keeping your mate happy and thankful you entered their life. In a world where things are constantly changing, be flexible to keep peace while understanding a new situation. There is nothing like true peace where it seems like every day just makes sense being together. Life should be joyous. Keep that smile on your mate's face. Having a comforting spirit helps in calming your mate in such a way that it's truly priceless. Being cheerful at times when the other person really needs that pick-me-up makes for a good moment. Be a good listener because this goes a long way for a great relationship.

Stay careful of each other's feelings and be mindful to keep love flowing through your heart to reciprocate back to your partner's heart as well. Focusing on all these ingredients makes for a special life together. It takes time to get all these things together just right. However, a lifetime is ahead so just take one day at a time. We can never be perfect, nevertheless doing your best to obtain excellence will get you an impeccable result. It's not about always being right all the time it's how you handle the obstacles and keep moving forward to make an unbelievable relationship be so fantastic.

When Later Date is Now

We have confidence in the Lord that you are doing and will continue to do the things we command.
2 Thessalonians 3:4, NIV

After Sophia and I started dating, six months later we were married. I'm sure there were people who said, "Whoa, that's fast!" However, each situation is different. Sometimes it is appropriate to slow things down, but you also have to know when to seize the opportunity. It's a feeling that only a man can feel on the inside. When we first started talking, I immediately felt a healing in my heart because I had been through so much. There was a great relief. It was such a blessing to be able to open my heart and talk to someone. But ultimately, it was the lead of God that connected us from the start.

I knew all about Sophia Ruffin. I knew her background. I knew her story, but her story was only one factor. I had a lot of internal issues to work through. My heart was damaged from the divorce, so I had to ask the Lord for guidance. What I was feeling for Sophia opened me up to a wave of new feelings. It was so amazing. I was feeling joy and peace once again. It changed my countenance. I was feeling and looking better. Even my mother noticed the newness in me. She'd see me in the house and ask, "You're happy, aren't you?" Yes, ma'am, I'm happy," I anxiously replied. I told my friends about Sophia. They were surprised and said, "Man, you just came out of a divorce. You're that serious about her already?" They didn't mean any harm, but they knew the mess I just got out of.

My belief is that a guy knows when he has found the right one. He can play if he wants, choose to mess around, or take his time, but I didn't want to. I wasn't going to string her along because that's just not right. I wanted something serious. She wanted something serious. It was time. And when the pieces came together, they fit so perfectly. So why wait? Why put it off? Why procrastinate and put it off for years? That doesn't make sense. You shouldn't do that to a woman, especially when you know she's the one for you. I knew what I wanted, and I knew what I needed. And that's why I say God knew what He was doing, but I had to step up to the plate and act on it.

Being in love is a serious situation. To be in love with someone who loves you back is so astounding. Often what people experience in relationships is superficial. Shallow relationships work for a while, but they don't last. True love has deep roots so it can withstand the storms of life and still be fruitful. I really thought I knew love, however being with Sophia made me reevaluate what true love is all about. Love makes you smile even when your mate is miles and miles away. Love will make you talk on the phone all night. Once, Sophia and I stayed on the phone for 10 hours and 28 minutes! That's longer than a workday! When love is the motivating factor, you will go out of your way to ensure everything is just right for the outing that you have planned. While you're making memories together, those experiences make your love grow stronger. Love isn't displayed by a string of grand gestures, but it's the little things that often count the most.

Don't despise small things because what seems to be small today could grow into something bigger. Sending love notes through text may seem small, however they work like a charm. Going throughout the day and then you think of your significant other, text a message of gratitude to them. With phones being so technologically advanced, sending a voice message is better than a text. With voice text messages, they can hear your message for themselves. Sometimes a text message can lack mood and emotion. Saying I love you is better than a heart emoji. That really makes them feel so special at that moment in time. It's the small expressions that last forever so why not use every moment to give your best. Sometimes you may not feel it but push through it. The excitement on your mate's face will say it all. Love will make you take photos and put them together that say something special on it.

Love will cause you to relocate. At first, I must admit it was quite difficult coming to Chicago during the cold winter. I found out why they call Chicago the "windy city." I learned new terminology like "wind chill factor" and "subzero temperature." I experienced that cold wind that can cut you like a knife. They call it "the hawk." Like I said, love will make you experience some new things. Thank God, we're not staying in Chicago!

Love is such a beautiful thing that the mere word doesn't do the experience justice. You must accept the trueness of the word. We haven't explored the word love to fathom its many facets. The love I feel right now is nothing I have felt in my life. It soothes my heart, body, and soul. My life has been turned upside down for the good, these last six months because love has made a new man out of me.

The Red Flags

*Jesus said to them: "Watch out that no one deceives you.
Mark 13:5, NIV*

Red flags are warning signs. In relationships red flags indicate that there is something wrong. A deeper problem is lurking beneath the surface. Red flags are to be seen but never ignored. They are to be heeded and paid attention to. Ignoring a red flag can be detrimental to the viability of any relationship. A major red flag for me was spirituality. If a person didn't believe in God, then we couldn't be in a relationship. The Bible is clear that we should not be unequally yoked together with unbelievers (2 Cor. 6:14).

If people have different belief systems and serve a different God, they are walking two different paths. Even if you are a Christian, all Christian denominations are not the same and interpret the Bible in different ways. So, a person can be a Christian, but you can still be unequally yoked. Therefore, you both need to attend a church where you both can serve the Lord together.

Another red flag is not being able to communicate and disagree in a non-combative way or becoming overly sensitive and argumentative. If she takes something simple out of context and becomes enraged over small things, that's a red flag. For example, if I believe one thing and she believes something different, we agree to disagree, move on and not end up in a fight. But if she always escalates to the next level, you're not going to get along. Life is hard enough. There's no sense having disagreements with someone you're not even in a relationship with yet. You're just getting to know each other. Nothing is perfect but at the same time, why start off that early with disagreements. It should be peaceful. It should be clean. It should be good.

No relationship is all peaches and cream. But we have to be careful of who we let speak over our marriages. We cannot be influenced by generalized comments by people who say, see if you get through the first five years. See if your marriage is still surviving after that. I understand that statistically twenty-five percent of marriages end in divorce within those first five years. However, I do not believe that we should make negative confessions over our marriages. That will never be my confession. My confession is my marriage is "for death do us part."

If she wants to go clubbing every weekend, that's a red flag. At the time, I was trying to get my money right, trying to get my health back and thinking long term for my children. Anything that was not pertaining to moving forward in life, anything that was going to cause unnecessary spending was a red flag. I didn't really have time for that. I was working during the week and trying to start my own business on the side. Then there was church and trying to get my mental and physical health together. So, anything that was taking me off course of where I needed to go, that was a red flag.

If a person is selfish and does not consider the needs of others, that's another red flag. I know we're two different people, two individuals, but be considerate. That's one thing I can say about Sophia. From the start, she was considerate and compassionate about my situation and what I had been through. I had people telling me, "You need to get off your butt and stop thinking about that," "Get over it," "You dropped the ball," "You fumbled," and all that. My reaction was okay, but you've never been in the situation so how can you tell me that I fumbled? You don't know what I went through. Talk is cheap. Never take advice from someone who has not been through what you are going through. That's like listening to a person who is advising you not to start your business, when they have never been in business.

Sophia never said anything like that. It was like she understood. That was an important check mark in her favor. When I told my friend Donald, even he said she was already a keeper, especially coming from someone of her status and what she has accomplished in life. Most women would never have given me a chance because of where I was at the time. I wouldn't be seen as a good catch. It was a huge deal for her to show compassion and to understand. She understood that I was trying to get my mental health right. She understood that I was seeing a therapist, trying to spend time with my kids, and let them know that everything was going to be alright. She spoke life into me from the beginning. Sure enough, on January 7, 2023, we solidified that.

Knowing your worth and striving to become the best version of yourself has to be the standard in your life. Without this you will settle for less and not get your best result. Why settle just because you made a mistake, or something didn't go as planned? Settling for less will stop your progress in reaching your goals in life. Mistakes are costly, however being down on yourself will keep you stuck. Time is so precious, but it doesn't wait for anyone. We must get to a point where our mind is set. The longer you wait in depression, denial, disappointment, discontentment you are losing time. You should be focused on developing, flourishing, thriving, maturing for your next chapter of your life. Just because one chapter ends badly, does not mean you should wallow in depression and breakdown.

These mishaps in life occur for a reason. Even something bad you can learn from. In other words, use that blunder to get yourself together, learn more about loving you and as a result of that allow the law of attraction to work in your favor. This is a powerful aspect that you can tap into. Positive thinking produces positive results in your natural life. So that being said start to think positively of the mate you really want in your life. This must be an intentional thing because it absolutely does work.

Think about this when you wake up in the morning with a happy go lucky attitude and it just seems like the day just goes by easily versus when you wake up with a negative demeanor. It's two different outcomes. The more you think about the positivity of what you want you start to attract that very thing you desire and deserve. So this ties into another important aspect in your life called your belief system. Have faith to believe in yourself and your ability to conquer no matter what you set out to accomplish, staying positive is a necessary component. Having this helps you stay the course when it seems to get a little gloomy. It's going to be rocky, however that's what makes it so worth it. You were built to withstand pain, disappointment, traumatizing incidents. The key is knowing it's only a test while enduring the bumps and bruises.

No matter how attractive someone may be, lowering your standards and expectations is not a good idea. Looks aren't everything. Your peace of mind is what counts. The moral compass you have is what matters the most. Your core beliefs will keep you grounded and on edge in knowledge of what you perceive. Listening to your inner self will help stir you away from the pitfalls that lie ahead. People will try to make you feel lesser because they need to down someone in order to lift themselves up. These types of people are nothing more than distractions. If you let them, they will drain you of your good energy to make themselves seem better. However, do not give them the time of day. Your game plan should always be to achieve a successful relationship, where love, being trustworthy, and understanding right from wrong, is the golden rule.

Here's a golden nugget. Never let someone tell you anything about dating or marriage if they haven't been married or been in a relationship. How can you help me when you haven't been to the place where I am going? How can you expect to be better when you're listening to one who is bitter? People who smile in your face sometimes don't have the right motives, be aware of such individuals. So, knowing your worth and who you are in God, will help you to never compromise your destiny.

DIFFERENCE BETWEEN DATE AND LATER DATE

*The fear of the LORD is the beginning of knowledge, but
fools despise wisdom and instruction.
Proverbs 1:7, NIV*

There's a difference between a date and later date. A date is something that is present or current. A later date is when you know you have something in mind for the future. I saw a future in Sophia even before we had the long conversations. There was just something about her. It was something that connected with my heart and spirit. It was the missing piece. Finding that missing piece was definitely the best day of my life, especially during that time. When you know you can spend the rest of your life with someone or you can see the potential of learning together, growing old together, traveling and all the other things that married couples do – that's when later date starts.

The later date is really securing something that is going to happen later when moving to the next phase. Later date doesn't mean no. It means not now. One of the biggest later date moments that stands out for me was the proposal. As we had conversations, later date was traveling together, going on trips and vacation. Later date was me cooking for her or just enjoying the day together. Later date was all the things that I wanted to make happen for us later. As you know, Sophia lives in Chicago so later date was being able to travel back to see my mom and my kids. Later date is so many scenarios. Waking up together was definitely a later date until we got married. Later date was going back to the restaurant where we had our first date, which we were able to do. Later date is so many things. If you put enough belief and faith in love, you will get what you want to come out of it. That's your later date.

It is important to pay close attention to detail while dating your mate. By being observant, it will be revealed how to treat and serve another. A watchful eye will be required because it will allow you to anticipate someone else's need before they ask. That's a good example of being connected. Being a servant is a quality that most people look down on. However, this person is vital because they help bring certain elements to a relationship. Everyone has strengths that need to be brought to the table for the goodness of the relationship.

Spending life together and knowing how to treat each other will make for a good future. There's nothing wrong with spoiling each other by understanding their wants and needs. Life is a teacher so learning the difference between these two is important. As individuals we want to be loved and feel love as well. That love is priceless when the right one comes along and applies that love. It's really a special feeling to have that love in your life. We want that love at some point in our life. Due to certain circumstances that have happened, you need that love. Needing love is normal because it fills a void that's been empty for so long. Don't get down in the dumps while in your waiting period because believing in love can provide substance to it. Just as in the natural when it rains afterwards a beautiful rainbow can appear. This is confirmation to you that bad will always happen but the good will come to outweigh the bad. Gloomy weather comes and goes, but they make the brighter days ahead even better.

Those days turned into weeks and then months. However, I knew that brighter days would eventually come. I keep telling myself it's going to be alright somehow. During this time, I was seeing a therapist because I knew I needed professional help sorting through my emotional issues. This helped me out tremendously and also knowing God was on my side was superb. Never forget who you're called to be in this world. There's greatness in everyone, the problem is some never tap into it. Even when my dark times came the light was there, but I couldn't see it. When these times come in your life talking with someone can help uncover the light. Confide in a person you trust; this will help your mental state in so many ways. These times require you to do the right thing for a future life that awaits you. In order to make it to the light, correct choices have to be made. Then you will discover that there is a bright future waiting ahead of you.

LATER DATE UNLOCKS PURPOSE

There is a time for everything, and a season for every activity under the heavens.
Ecclesiastes 3:1, NIV

Later Date is also helping to unlock the purpose in one another. That's why it's important to marry the right person. It's very crucial because he who finds a wife, finds a good thing, and obtains favor and blessings from God. Favor is the unlocking. Favor is the blessings. Favor is the accomplishments that you will do together, and it's also the pouring into each other. It's knowing each other. Even though I know Sophia is an ambassador and a prophet, it's me speaking into my wife what God is saying at times that adds to her. That's what she needs from me. That's a healthy relationship.

People will always have their opinions, but I'm not concerned about what anyone else says. It doesn't concern me because after all that we have been through, it's nothing to God. He knows what he wants to do for you. He wants to do more than you can even think. I just thank God for all the family that has supported me during this time. I'm thankful for those who have said that not only do I deserve it, but we deserve it as a couple because they know Sophia's story. I'm thankful for the many people that have witnessed what they've witnessed, seen what they've seen and heard what they've heard. At the end of the day in my wife's words, "It will be God, or it will be God."

God will place you where you need to be in life. In other words, he will arrange the circumstances for the best outcome according to His plan for you. So, in my experience I was afraid of failure and almost let that hinder my endeavor in writing. But as I look back to see where I came from, it's a testament that God can transform any situation. I'm being transparent because I want to help people learn from what I had to go through for a good purpose. Had I not gone through my darkest moments, this book would never have been written. So it was my destiny for me to sustain the pain and suffering for a brief time, so I could get back up to write this book.

God never tells us how it will be down the line; we just have to trust the process of knowing He's in total control. Now I never knew a book was going to be birthed out of me, but in my lowest moments it was being stirred up. But here's where the favor was being released even before I had any clue. Sophia has written several books and has a writing class for individuals. So, looking back at it now, I realize her expertise was sent for a particular purpose. While getting to know each other and talking during these times, Sophia's proficiency helped guide me. I had to lean on her belief system so that I could write a book. I didn't think I could do it.

It is essential that you have someone who pushes greatness out of your life. Don't be scared to step out and do something different. You will be surprised at the result. Under those circumstances where uncertainty exists, have faith. A phenomenal concept that could revolutionize the world is one idea away. Your gift is not only for you, because it could have a worldwide impact. You are a powerful global being with a purpose.

Husband Material

And we know that in all things God works for the good of those who love him, who have been called according to his purpose.
Romans 8:28, NIV

I've heard people say that God prepares a woman to be a wife, and in a sense, she's a wife before she meets her husband. But I also make this statement about me: Tommy is a husband. Other people have made this statement about me too. That's because they know the type of person I am, and they know my character. They know how I treat a lady. They have watched me over the years. People who have been friends with me for a while know about me. My character will go before me because of who I am and my integrity. That's something that I pride myself in.

I always say that I get that from my parents, my upbringing of just being a good person and treating everybody with respect. But also going a little bit above and beyond when you can doesn't hurt. That's what the world needs more of; more love, more compassion, more character, more integrity, more doing the right thing even when no one is watching.

So, me, Tommy Wilson, I'm husband material. I know what it takes, and I have wisdom in that area. That's what makes it great for me. And it's what's going to make it great for us, for me and my wife.

How to love in uncertainty is very important to a healthy relationship. First too many people have been hurt to the core to where love is not admitted. In order to be loved you must forgive the ones who did the wrong. Hurt is a crucial element to get over and move on. It's like a nagging headache that will not go away. Always keep a positive attitude about love entering your life again. Without this thought it will be hard to attract the love you desire and deserve. I know it's hard to let your guard down when so many play games these days. Discernment is not only a must but a requirement to your success in determining your mate.

Dating is good because it allows you to see how you get along, it helps you understand the dynamics of each other and learn about that individual. It seems easy but it is work involved so that you really interpret actions over feelings. Feelings are inconsistent and can cloud judgment, but actions let you know how serious a person is about you. True intentions are backed by actions that will solidify the motives. A person can talk all day, but can they back it up with action. There's nothing worse than not following through on what you said you're going to do. Saying you are going to do something has no impact. What you do is what counts, not what you say.

There is a saying that I find useful, "under promise and over deliver." This is a wise saying to live by. In a relationship you have to go over and beyond giving your all to please your mate. To keep your promises will keep a smile on your partner's face while giving you satisfaction. You have to remind yourself that your best is coming. It's not thinking more highly of yourself, you just do not want to settle for just anything. Circumstances in life will beat you down and tell you that this is all you're going to get. No, should be your answer. The good news is that every day can be great with the right person in your life. We all deserve to be loved in such a way that you get goosebumps thinking about it. Keep your heart open for a love that will knock you off your feet. It's out there for you.

Marriage is simply not the day you said, "I Do." It's a lifetime commitment of daily pledges to do and be better and constantly changing or growing. However, you see it needs to be done on both sides. If one is evolving daily and the other person is not, this is the basis for conflict. Enlarging yourself while your partner is in your shadow can be disastrous. One cannot always be strong for both of you. Carrying the burden for two is not healthy.

Growing together is an absolute must, because when both individuals grow together it only strengthens the bond between both of you. Doing certain things together is essential to keep that love flowing. Most people think that the gifts, clothes, eating out and material things is what attracts a person. It's the intangible things like, being considerate, being a gentleman, it's about doing the right thing when no one else is watching. Life is a great teacher, so I'm just giving my tips to help. This blissful season right now came through a rough time however look at me now. To God be the glory. Remember to treat your mate with kindness at all times because they deserve it.

GIVE LOVE ANOTHER CHANCE

In this way they will lay up treasure for themselves as a firm foundation for the coming age, so that they may take hold of the life that is truly life.
1 Timothy 6:19, NIV

Don't be afraid to give love another chance. Just because you were hurt, or something happened in the past doesn't mean it's going to happen again. Don't be afraid to try one more time. You have to go back to when you first started learning how to ride a bike. You fell several times but that didn't stop you. You kept trying. That's exactly how it is in life. Don't let past failure deter you from starting all over again. There's nothing wrong with trying again. That's what makes us human. That's what life is all about.

You have to give love your all and not let one or more incidents stop you from attaining love like you want in life. There is someone out there for everyone. You just must find that one that's for you. Yes, I went through something traumatic, and I didn't want to go through that again. But God said, that's not so. You can't determine what your life is going to be because of that incident, because of what you've been through. That's only going to make you stronger for the next time. It will make you wiser for that next go around. You just have to go through the pain to learn for your future.

So does love have to be a roller coaster of emotions? Well, my answer is love is what you make of it. The ups and downs are just a prerequisite for your love to be tested. Proving what love is and how it is in your relationship is just what I call learning phases. We have heard about love and we have seen love firsthand growing up. However, when you are in a relationship, your love is the real deal. You can learn about love in books and see how it is recognized on television, but when it's your life then love is totally different. You want to put love on display and make it so personal to you. There's nothing wrong with doing so because having love for someone is a privilege. The ability to love plus have love for someone hits so hard to your heart. The interaction on how love makes you feel and how your heart is connected to someone is so powerful.

Love can be so many things in a good relationship, that's why everyday should be a blessing to be with your special one. When you have been hurt or wronged in any way, the day you find that one love that hits all points, just know that's special. So, you have to be real with yourself and say love will come my way. Being selfish at this point can be the turning point that attracts what you want. Love can come directly to you when you least expect it. Pray for it, seek it out, learning about yourself will help you be ready for your love. Being ready for love is crucial rather than trying to get ready for love. I heard a song called Lessons and it helped me in so many ways. I used to listen to it on repeat, that's how therapeutic it was to me. It basically said that all I have been through led me up to you and thank God, he directed me this way. Life is a journey, and we must learn along the way while living our lives. Take the lesson and learn as much as you can from that experience. I have learned so much that now love has new meanings and definitely new memories that will last for a lifetime. So make your own meaning of love with your partner with a new heart.

Life is so good when you are with the one designed exactly for you. So when you really love someone you will understand why it's important to give your love to the right one. Love shouldn't be handed out to everyone it needs to be appreciated by the one who deserves that special love. Be careful with your heart, it shouldn't be played with. You must have good discernment these days because it's a lot of people out here with tricks. So how do know if someone is telling the truth about themselves? If their words don't line up with their actions, then something is wrong. Experience has taught me that when life gets tough, and you don't know your next step trust God no matter what.

Getting past the darkest times in your past will be difficult at first but keep making new memories as you go. Day by day you'll find yourself feeling better and stronger because you are thinking about positive outcomes for your life. These times that come to get you down must come but use this as a motivation to keep striving for the life you want.

Roadblocks will always be there, however there's always another way to get to your destination. So, it's truly how you perceive yourself that matters to the future you. The choices you make today can change your life forever. When life hits you sit back and check your balance so your mind can focus on what's important. By doing this, when opposition comes it will help you stay the course because now you know why. The why is important because it keeps you grounded and helps you realize your purpose. Keeping the why at the forefront of your mind helps inform your next moves so they can be critical to obtaining your heart's desires.

Love is the object of every relationship and should be demonstrated on a daily basis. We shouldn't fall out of love when things are not going the way we want them to go. You must still show love and grace to your partner because we're not all together ourselves. Learn to love through all even when you might be upset or mad. Never make your partner feel as though they made a horrible mistake by accepting the person you are.

As life goes on, we must still love each other when adverse things in life happen to us. Getting past difficult times without turning on one another or splitting up helps solidify our relationships. Don't overlook this mark in life. These are situations where dialogue amongst two individuals must be carried out. Love will carry you during your toughest times, due to it being such a powerful force. It's such a powerful feeling to have love in your life and especially when it overtakes your heart. Love is special and I pray you find that love that will make you say I must be dreaming.

Day 19

How I Met My Wife

But God demonstrates his own love for us in this: While we were still sinners, Christ died for us.
Romans 5:8, NIV

I first met Sophia in 2017, when she preached at my church, Greater Grace Houston. I was armor bearer for Apostle E. L. Usher and doing security that night as well. I was on my post and Sophia came out of the room. First Lady Tawanda Usher introduced us and that was it. In brief passing I said my name and nice to meet you, and then was back on my job. Five years later in 2021, Sophia came back to the church, but I was going through my divorce situation. I heard her preaching and remembered meeting her a few years back.

Once my divorce was final, I asked the First Lady to inquire and ask what and how she was doing. First Lady Usher said, "Great', let me call her." Lady Usher called her, and within seconds we were connected on a three-way call. We talked for about a good thirty minutes, then First Lady said, "I think y'all got this. You just need to exchange numbers." We did that, and then I called Sophia right back to talk some more. The rest is history. We got to know each other. I let her know up front what I was going through and what I'd been through. I laid everything on the line, not realizing that both my needs and my wants were being filled right then.

I was taking it slow. I wasn't trying to rush into something because I didn't know what would come from this. However, I thank God that day happened. I thank God that everything that I've been through led up to the blissful space that we're in right now. We talked on the phone for two weeks. Then on June 24, 2022, Sophia came back to my church to speak at the *W.O.W. Conference*. We planned our first date, not realizing that was the start of everything. That was the day that my heart was truly at ease. It was at peace, and it was totally healed just by us going out. We didn't know it would turn into a proposal, a marriage, and all that. We just knew we were having fun. It was a good time.

Of course, being the man that I am, I did what I was supposed to do. I set up everything correctly from the personalized menus at the restaurant where we ate dinner to a special gift with rose petals. That's the way she should be treated no matter what was going to come from that date. It was just a man showing a woman how she should be treated. And that's what I did.

I never thought a long-distance relationship would ever work for me. It seemed that it could be taxing on each other and would take more effort to make it work. I wasn't sure how it would work out, but here's what happened. One day while Sophia and I were talking on the phone she suggested that I should experience a Chicago winter. I'll never do that, I responded. However, little did I realize that indeed I would be catching flights to Chicago during the winter. The moral of the story, be careful what you say you're not going to do. Since my love lived in Chicago, I had to endure the winter up there. Yes, it gets very cold in Chicago, but my baby was in Chicago and wherever she was, That's where I wanted to be.

Being apart actually gave us something to look forward to. It made it so special when we saw each other. Those in between times when we weren't together made our love grow stronger. Now I understand the saying that "absence makes the heart grow fonder." In reality, the cold in Chicago wasn't the issue, it was my mindset about the cold that was the real issue. Having the right attitude can help determine how things turn out. So often we build up ideas that are not true. Besides, we have technology that can assist when we are away from our loved ones. Try Face Time, Zoom or other apps that facilitate live video communication. Be innovative. Since I know Sophia loves basketball, I made a flier that requested her time to watch the NBA finals as a virtual date.

So little gestures are so good for a relationship. It's the thought that counts. A simple gift with thoughtful love note helps keep the flame of passion burning even when you are away from each other. Then there's always the grand gestures that have a bigger impact to the heart, but be strategic with those, such as special occasions. However, do whatever you can to convey that you care. Big or small, when it's from the heart your mate will definitely appreciate it. Love is so complex and simple at the same time. That's what makes getting to know each other so significant. It's about making memories together that helps build a strong connection with love.

It is important to know what your mate likes. Like a textbook, you must study your mate. We all have different personalities so understanding will help you accommodate future activities. Careful planning keeps things that are on the horizon come together for a great union. As the anticipation grows before a trip to see Sophia, I actually get a little nervous, because it's like I'm seeing her for the first time. The feeling I experienced when we finally saw each other again, truly took my breath away.

So, how did I know Sophia was the one? Did it all come about quickly? My testimony is, when you know, you just know. Let's unpack this first question. Honestly, a man knows when he has truly found the one. It's a feeling deep down in your soul. It's like you only see that one individual in a crowd of people. It's true, there are countless prospects in the world. However, when you find that special someone, then that's what makes it special. From the very beginning, I knew I wasn't going to play around with someone else's heart. I definitely knew Sophia was not messing around either. I was on a mission. I understood my assignment. Besides, at this stage of my life I wanted to be upfront and honest with Sophia.

An important aspect of our relationship is that there was a connection before the power of our relationship was turned on. Just as an electrician must lay out the wiring properly before a circuit is energized, so it was in the beginning of our relationship. We established good communication and started corresponding which helps to drown out any interference. Sometimes our conversations were simple, asking how your day was or talking about something that was humorous. We must learn to appreciate the simple things in life.

With Sophia in my life, I can operate in a capacity to fulfill my purpose. There was a deep aspiration to be with someone that appreciates who I am and who I can become. So, as we kept talking on the phone our relationship developed. One day, there was a conference being hosted at my church Greater Grace there in Houston. Sophia was one of the speakers. It was suggested by my First Lady Tawanda Usher to set a dinner after her preaching engagement. So, the wheels started turning immediately. I started thinking about restaurants to go to and how I wanted everything to be special. I found a place in the Galleria of Houston with the right romantic environment and ambiance. I had the menus printed out and went to *Office Depot* to have *S.R. (for Sophia Ruffin) June 24, 2022, First Date in H-town* printed on the menu. I couldn't stop there, so I got a canvas painting of some Jordan 1's put it in a nice gift bag and with some fresh rose petals to set a romantic atmosphere.

So, after Sophia preached, we headed to the restaurant where I made all the preparations. So, I pulled up in our car and used the valet parking. We entered the restaurant, and I told them my name and they escorted us to our table. Two minutes later, I had arranged the hostess to bring our personalized menus and her gift to the table with Sophia's gift placed right beside her. At first glance, it just looked like a regular menu until Sophia saw the personalized heading.

Her face said it all! She put her hand in the bag and pulled out a couple of red rose petals. She asked, "are these real?" "Yes, they are," I replied. I wanted to be intentional on everything that night so she will always remember that magical night. With all this excitement going on I'm literally so nervous just wanting everything to be perfect. We then ordered our food, and it was exquisite.

This date was special in so many ways because I knew then I was going to ask her hand in marriage. As I sat on the other side of the table and just smiling back and forth. I knew then Sophia was the one I wanted and needed. I went out of my way for a reason to show I cared for, her. I wanted her to know how a man should treat her. Just to see the look on her face was priceless simply a beautiful smile did it for me. It was such a beautiful night that we didn't want it to end. However, Sophia was heading out Saturday morning so, I took her back to the hotel. I got out and opened her door and we shared an intense loving gaze. Then we hugged each other and I said "I truly enjoyed every moment of our time tonight and can't wait until our next date." The feeling was mutual, and I knew at that point I wanted to spend life with her. To keep it very respectful, I kissed her on the cheek. To have set all this up and it went just as planned let's me know right then a there this is the start of something great.

The proposal on the other hand was a tricky situation because this had to be a total surprise to Sophia. I say tricky because her team knew exactly what I was planning without spilling the beans. I simply wanted everything to go smoothly so when the moment came it would be an emotional moment, happy tears and all. Let's dive in about getting this ring to start things off. In general conversation I asked Sophia what type of ring she likes? Her response was something simple yet elegant. Great, now I know what to look for.

One Friday morning I woke up and got dressed to proceed to pick out her ring. I was simply going to look and get some prices to know about how much they would be. I get to one jeweler I'm looking at all of these diamond rings all of them sparkling so bright. I picked out two of them and compared them. To help make a decision, I got opinions from the staff. The first one I picked was the absolute best choice from what Sophia likes. When I saw the price tag I thought, yep that's definitely a nice ring! I knew this was a very expensive purchase, but it comes with a lifetime of love attached to it. So, it was worth every penny.

The salesperson said let's run your credit. That's where I became nervous. I was thinking, "oh boy here we go." Mind you, I'm recently divorced and trying to get back on my feet financially. But at the same time, I just believed God, that everything will work out according to His plan. The salesperson presented a few options for me to see what's best for my situation. While I'm sitting down waiting for the result of my credit check, the person comes in and says, "I've got good news, you've been approved." Whew, that was a big relief. My heart leaped for joy. Immediately Sophia's favorite song starts to play in the background. So, I started recording myself walking around so she could hear her song, but not let her know the store where I was shopping. I was approved for the ring plus more, so I walked out with the ring in hand. Now onto planning the proposal.

To plan a proposal that will make Sophia's day was the goal for me. I had to navigate through key people in Sophia's circle to get numbers to plan a grand proposal that will take her breath away. The first thing I had to get accomplished was to get her dad's blessing to marry his daughter. I'm for doing things the right way and in order. When I called Sophia's dad, I was nervous, but I had confidence in myself. As I picked up my phone to make the call, a calmness came over me. One minute later I'm talking to her dad telling him I love his daughter so much that I want to ask her to marry me so we can spend our lives together. I asked him for his blessing, and he said I'm so proud to have this moment happening. His reply was, "yes you have my blessing." I said thank you, and that she will be in good hands because I know how to treat her and she deserves the goodness of a great man who puts God first.

So, after I got that off my plate, there were so many more things to do for this proposal to come through correctly. Where, when, and how are the thoughts going through my mind. I have the ring in my possession, now how long do I hold it and where should I propose to her? There were so many questions and so few answers. That's when I called my best friend since the sixth grade, for advice about planning the proposal. I even consulted with my pastor, Bishop Usher about this so I could make the best decision. After considering both perspectives, it helped me realize when it's done from the heart, Sophia will be overwhelmed by my genuine efforts to make this a grand event.

I intentionally wanted every moment to be just right on that day. At first, I thought about proposing on Christmas Day.

However, I know I couldn't wait that long. So, I decided on proposing during the conference that was coming up. I knew a lot of very important people close to her were going to be there. The special ones who have been there with you during the rough times deserve to share this special moment.

As I stated earlier there was a lot of planning and coordination that went into this event. Nevertheless, Sophia's team had to keep her out of the loop this whole time and they did an excellent job. Admittedly, I was a nervous wreck knowing what's about to happen at this event. I love to give surprises, and this was definitely one that had to go off without a hitch. I say that because this is Sophia's moment that will stick with her for the rest of her life. So as the proposal date drew closer, I was trying to keep my composure. But in the midst of all the coordination and orchestration I would stop to give God the glory for allowing me to be at the doorsteps of marriage once again. To get a chance to ask this esteemed woman of God, for her hand in marriage was simply fantastic. However, even though I already had her dad's blessing, there was one more person who I needed to speak with. While I was in Chicago for the conference, I had to get the man of God's blessing, the Apostle.

While at the airport ready to board the plane to Chicago for the conference, my phone rang. On the phone was Apostle John Eckhardt. "Is this Tommy" he asked, Yes, it is, how may I help you today," I replied. This caught me by surprise, but I was glad he called. At that point I simply said, "Apostle I love Sophia so much and I want to propose to her at the conference on the first night will that be okay?" "That sounds good" he replied. Thank you, sir, I said with a smile. So, with that out the way, now I'm ready now to get to Chicago. Now my intensity level has elevated to high. I'm contemplating what I'm going to say when I propose. I was nervous because I didn't know how she would react to this. I know some have probably asked, how do you know she will say yes? I was positive because from the very beginning the foundation was laid correctly. And when you find your missing piece, it just fits perfectly. I have never been in love like this before and it feels so good. The feelings I have towards Sophia are so saturated with love that just the thought of what we have brings great fulfillment.

Now comes September 29, 2022, a surprising day to remember. As the hours draw closer my heart is racing and I am just excited to see Sophia's face when I drop on one knee. I had so many people in my corner saying they were extremely happy about what is unfolding right now. So, service starts, and everyone has kept it all together and I couldn't be more thankful for that. When Sophia walks onto the stage, she brings up Apostle Eckhardt. Then I get into position. I got the flowers and mic in hand, but that's where everything went blank. It happened so quickly. I said Sophia, when you came into my life everything changed. I had been saying later date, but later date is now. I then proceeded to kneel down on one knee and pull out the ring. My next words were Sophia Nicole Ruffin will you please marry me. With such excitement and emotion all over here face she said, yes! Her response truly made me a happy man. My baby said yes to me, and it was like the whole room was filled with tears, joy, happiness, and pure love. That feeling was amazing and I'm so grateful to all that played a part in helping me that day and leading up to that moment.

So as the wedding day drew closer, the level of excitement and anticipation increased by the moment. It's wonderful to know that we will be married very soon. It's so many levels to process and keep your composure as you go about your day. The opportunity to be in covenant with someone you get along with, cherish spending time together and enjoy loving one another is something so special and rewarding. Married to me means loving someone from head to toe not caring about others' opinions or beliefs. You are two people coming together as one to create a bond that lasts forever. These are the moments that make all the disappointments worth celebrating together. All good things happen in time so just wait for your best to come your way.

Love Factor

*He who finds a wife finds what is good
and receives favor from the LORD.
Proverbs 18:22, NIV*

It was so hard to contain so much excitement from all that's going on. It seemed so sudden, from getting to know Sophia one minute, to planning an engagement, then a wedding, the next minute. God has a way of speeding things up. At first, hope seemed to be a long way off. While I was going through, my trials that led to my divorce seemed to take forever. But now that God has put Sophia in my life it's like He made haste to bring our marriage to pass. In life you're put on display so someone can see how you made it out of a terrible spot. We both have endured some tough moments in life, but we don't look like what we have gone through. That's the evidence of a great victory, coming out without any wounds. What has happened in the past is behind us now. We're both moving together with our hearts in sync to continue to be overcomers.

There was so much to coordinate. What we already had in front of us was already overwhelming, but then a magazine called us to feature us in a future edition. So, they're covering the engagement and the wedding. It's such an honor to be given celebrity status where we would be videotaped and take photos for this magazine. Through being published in this magazine our story will touch so many lives. It's so humbling to be able to give glory to God. When you plant good seeds expect that you will reap a blessed crop. Our love for each other has been so strong and genuine that others can see it, and experience it through the pictures and videos on social media. This is not a mere show for the camera, this is real love at its best.

It's wonderful to be in love with someone who has your back. Love will give you a peace when chaos is all around you. Love will change your perspective on life that nothing can stop you now. Love will put a smile on your face just thinking about how much you adore your mate. Love will heal emotional wounds from the past. Love will usher in the favor and blessing that has been held up from the bondage of the past. Love will overcome obstacles that arise to block positive outcomes. Love shall be a standard for the solid foundation on which we stand. Love is it, love is the key, love is all. Love is respect, love is being there at all costs. Love is knowing that your love will not be deterred. Love is growing and understanding each other. This is what I call the Love Factor.

Your love should be focused. Centering your love will help maneuver through the ups and downs of life situations. You have to be patient with yourself and keep moving on to a joyful life. We all have things that get under our skin. However, it's your response that determines what happens next. How you acknowledge a lesson will help your future steps in life. Love must be true. Artificial love will not last, nor can it be the grounds to keep a couple together.

Trying to force a person to love you will not work. Coming together has to be a natural progression between the two sides. Building something with a strong foundation is the key to thriving a relationship. If you're not moving towards the goals that you set, then what are you doing? Love has to be meaningful. It's like building a house from the ground up, every room must have a purpose and meet certain design specifications. So, with a relationship, it must be built to withstand the stress of life. Why design a relationship that will fail? Pay attention to your relationship. Inspecting attentively from the ground floor up is imperative and should not be taken lightly. It may take time as you oversee your love project, and it's not easily built, but I guarantee that the process will be worth all the effort.

What do you do when things don't feel right, or tension is in the air? First of all, you must come together and talk to each other. Not talk at each other. Someone must have a cool enough head to take down and listen. Both sides have a point of view that must be acknowledged, whether you agree with them or not. When you fail to hear the other person's side, then they will not listen to your side either. When that happens problems cannot be resolved. The thoughtfulness of each other's feelings should be demonstrated in a loving manner. There are always two sides to each story.

Each person's feelings and perspective should be taken into consideration. That's how healthy communication is conducted. Life will definitely throw things to get you off kilter. Knowing this, allows you to anticipate when potential problems can arise.

Giving space to one another gives the other person the ability to blow off steam. Maybe writing down your thoughts on the subject can help ease your mind and even taking a walk outside will give some clarity. What works for you can be a lot of things, just know your heaviness will be lifted. It's sure not easy to be in these times together however successful relationships are forged through the conflicts that you resolve together. Remember, these days will come, just make sure they go by quickly. Do not let the sun go down on your wrath. In other words, try not to go to bed angry with one another. Forgiving one another is key for a loving relationship and even a peaceful night of sleep.

The focus should be that your relationship will be enjoyable. Your rewards are coming from the Lord above who has brought you together, therefore let no one pull you apart. Just stay the course and keep inching towards your peacefulness. When tears come to you wipe them away and say it's just clearing my vision for the future. The only way to make it better than ever is by believing that God has a plan for your marriage. Stay in the right frame of mind. If you don't believe in your marriage, it cannot be successful. Once I cleared my mind of the clutter and disappointment, I saw a brighter day ahead and I was ready to pursue Sophia when we came across each other's path.

Seeing yourself in a good place first is significant to your belief system. Building up this confidence will help make your core strengthen to the maximum extent. This kind of inner strength will be seen by your peers as you emerge. This is powerful for you, but your display of perseverance will be a benefit to so many others. This kind of thing is what's needed in a world that is very doubtful. Positivity is not just needed it's necessary.

Final Thoughts

And so we know and rely on the love God has for us. God is love. Whoever lives in love lives in God, and God in them.
1 John 4:16, NIV

In this book, I share many important aspects of our relationship with you. I'm thankful for my wife, for encouraging me to write this book. I never knew I had it in me. This has been a journey, because I had to live out in real-time what I have written about, yet it's truly been an honor. In life you never know what you are going to end up doing. First being married to an awesome woman, and now, an author. Wow, what a mighty God we serve. It has been truly humbling.

Our lives have been more on display since the proposal and it's exciting to hear all the good feedback. It's really a good thing to hear that people love our story. To be involved in this awesome experience. Just to hear that friends and family are here to support and celebrate our union overwhelms me with joy. I'm so proud to marry such a beautiful woman that has a heart to match. I cherish my wife and God's favor on our lives.

Live life to the fullest is my motto. Sophia in my life makes this statement more personal. Good things come to those who wait, keep going because your dreams can appear right before you. I think we represent something special that love can do if you allow yourself to heal from hurt to obtain happiness and joy. This is why getting past obstacles that hinder your faith in love is necessary to achieve such a successful love story. You deserve to have a love that will make you a happy individual for life.

January 7, 2023, was a great vibe. It was a day to remember. Our wedding day was magical to say the least and went off so well it seemed scripted. The day before was the wedding rehearsal with the bridal party and it was a time of business and celebration for us. It was a lot of fun and plenty of laughs with everyone. The atmosphere was so nice and warm, literally it felt like something out of the movies. As we walked through our positions a couple of times with the party it was time to eat. The dinner was at a very nice restaurant and the bridal party loved that. We had a good time of fellowship, and some gave us our flowers by words of encouragement. So thoughtful and generous of them to share their stories about us. This was my last time seeing Sophia until the ceremony and it was hard to say goodbye to her. I knew I would see her tomorrow, but it was going to be something to see her in that dress for the first time. The anticipation was growing and knowing people were coming in from all over was just so amazing. Family, friends flying and driving in to witness our wedding had me so overjoyed. It really means a lot to have individuals come supporting us like this.

Me being in the men's quarters adjacent to the chapel, I could see all the vehicles pulling into the parking lot. It was filling up quickly. Just to think people have taken time out their schedules to be here at the Royal Wedding, as I found out that someone posted on Facebook as R plus W joining in union. I was so happy to see family members that I haven't seen in years just smiling away in the chapel to the reception. Everything was so beautiful and the comments about the whole experience were tremendously inspiring. We wanted everyone to have a wonderful experience on our special day. You can only hope for everything to go right on a day like this. The vision was given to our wedding planner, and she followed it. Therefore, the ceremony was all that and more. The bride is the only one that matters because it's her dream that must take place that day. Everything leading to this point is so crucial. Indeed, this was a big production.

Waking up that Saturday morning knowing I'm getting married in a couple of hours was so meaningful. It's like I was floating on cloud nine. I was so ready to say I do. The feeling I have for Sophia is so very strong that I could feel it all through my body and heart. Sophia changed me as a man and I'm so grateful to her. Getting dressed for this wedding with my groomsmen was an experience that taught me family and friends matter so much. Through it all, I'm so glad I kept pushing myself to get better and it definitely worked out. Reminiscing about life together and understanding others' lives make this day so memorable.

I'm finally dressed and walking with my best man and best friend since six grade to go take our first touch pictures was priceless. I had butterflies. I was so nervous yet knowing it's all going to be okay. Once I'm in the main house they blind folded me. My best friend had to guide me up the stairs. That was a real lesson concerning having the right people in your life is needed. I had to trust someone else to lead me while I was in the dark. It's a good feeling knowing I was in good hands heading upstairs to take these photos.

Touching Sophia's hand sent chills all over my body. Just knowing my future wife was right there was thrilling. I loved everything about that picture session before we said I do. The moment was a wonderful experience that words cannot describe. It was an experience that people will never forget. I say that because I was a part of a wedding that love, excitement, gratitude, gracefulness, joy, happiness, everyone felt throughout the whole ceremony. To have so many people come together and celebrate with us was truly overwhelming with joy.

Seeing Sophia walking down the aisle with her dad, I did tear up because she was absolutely beautiful and elegant. I was thinking I'm so blessed to be able to marry her. My mind was at ease when she finally made it to the altar as I took her hand. The ceremony was so beautiful and when we said "I do," it was lights out let's get this party started. I say that, to say this; after everything Sophia and I have been through this last year we deserve to party and enjoy ourselves for coming out on top. To God be the glory for this grand occasion and all the blessings he has bestowed upon us. I'm so thankful for the photographers and videographers to capture all these spectacular memories. Seeing the reception venue for the first time was jaw dropping it was done with elegance and pizazz. We couldn't make it to the big house where our special guest saxophonist was entertaining our guest. We heard he put on a grand show, and we are extremely grateful for him. Like I said this was a professional production that went on like a Royal Wedding.

Our entrance into reception was amazing. Being introduced as Mr. and Mrs. Wilson was very sentimental. Let me tell you. I was in a zone, and I couldn't come out. Walking down the aisle was surreal. I did tear up when I saw Sophia approaching the altar. She was so beautiful wearing that spectacular wedding dress. Like a scene out of a movie, her dad proudly escorted her in. It was dreamlike knowing later on we would be celebrating with everyone in attendance.

It really seemed to take a long time for her to enter the room, however when she did, I will never forget it. The joy of seeing her in her dress for the first time was truly breathtaking. She was so exquisite and ravishing in her dress, like straight out of a dream. Just knowing that we had a great wedding planner who single-handedly pulled off the wedding of the century was so beneficial to us. The whole day was a big production, and it was run at the next level. The first time being introduced as Mr. and Mrs. Wilson felt so good to hear. Walking in together was one for the books. Holding hands and dancing was everything for me. Our chemistry from the beginning has been on point and now that we're married will continue to grow stronger. What a feeling to know I found my missing piece. Now life is blissful.

It is my prayer that after reading this book, and hearing my story that forgiveness is released from your heart from past hurt, and that you will give love a chance again. I pray that you will experience *Later Date* and will live the blissful life GOD has planned for you.

The End

ABOUT THE AUTHOR

TOMMY WILSON JR. is a dedicated father to his three adult children. He has been active in the church for decades and is a loyal member of Greater Grace Church of Houston, Texas. He has served as the armour bearer to Apostle E. L. Usher accompanying him on numerous meetings and speaking engagements. His past experiences paved the way for his current role in traveling around the world with his wife Prophetesses and Ambassador Sophia Ruffin. With the debut of his new book, Tommy is now a sought-after personality speaking at conferences and conventions throughout the nation and the world.

Follow Tommy at:

Facebook	Tommy Wilson
Instagram	tdub1414
TikTok	@tommywilson97

ABOUT THE PUBLISHER

Let *Life to Legacy* bring your story to literary life! We offer the following publishing services: manuscript development, editing, transcription services, ghost-writing, cover design, copyright services, ISBN assignment, worldwide distribution, and eBook conversion.

Throughout production, we keep the author informed every step of the way. Even if you do not have a manuscript, that's not a problem for us. We can ghost-write your book from audio recordings or legible handwritten documents. Whether print-on-demand or trade publishing, we have packages to meet your publishing needs. At *Life to Legacy*, we take the stress out of becoming a published author.

Unlike other *so-called* publishers, we do more than just print books. Our books and eBooks are distributed to book buyers, distributors, and online retailers throughout the world—this is real publishing! Call us today for a free quote.

Please visit our website
www.Life2Legacy.com
or call us
708-272-4444

Send e-mail inquiries
Life2Legacybooks@att.net

www.ingramcontent.com/pod-product-compliance
Lightning Source LLC
Chambersburg PA
CBHW032131090426
42743CB00007B/552